Thin Black Road
And Other Inspirational Christian Poems

By Julie C. Gilbert

Love Science Fiction or Mystery?

Choose your adventure!
Visit: **http://www.juliecgilbert.com/**

For details on getting free books.

Dedication:

For my friends Jenny Parsons and Marie Graham.

Table of Contents:

Introduction:

Dear reader,

I've tried organizing these poems a few dozen different ways. What you see is what I believe to be the most logical order. I've tried putting the inspirational ones first followed by the stories. At first, I had them in the order they were written with the dates listed, but I've come to realize that most people won't know or care about specific dates being associated with certain poems. Besides, it made me feel old to realize how long ago some of them were written. On the other hand, if you're ever curious, feel free to email me (**devyaschildren@gmail.com**) and I can attempt to tell you what lay behind a certain poem.

Each poem is a song.

Most were written while I was in college. Some have been published in other stories, such as the Heartfelt Cases series. Where applicable, I will list the work you can find the poem in.

Hope you enjoy them. Let me know your thoughts. I enjoy getting to know people.

Sincerely,

Julie C. Gilbert

1. Thin Black Road

There's a thin black road
I have traveled many times.
It leads to peace
In so many ways.
It's kind of hard to describe
For the road's oft unclear.
It unfolds to me
Like a lovely gift
One word at a time.
Then, music fills in the gaps,
Making worries fade away,
As unexplainable peace pours in.
There's a thin black road
It leads me to peace.
When good or ill tidings come
To threaten my equilibrium,
I will travel that road
And return to peaceful calm.

2. Burden Not Seen

Here is the anthem of my soul:
Only the Lord can make me whole.

God, I am asking you to set me free;
I have a burden others cannot see.

I have a need to help out somewhere,
But I need you to take me there.

Lift me up with Holy hands;
Help me pull others from sinking sands.

Give me all the right words to say,
And all this, in your name I'll pray.

For I have a burden others cannot see,
And only you, O Lord, can set me free.

3. To My Former Master

Dear Former Master, listen well,
I am no longer bound for Hell.
Can you not see?
You have no power over me!

I have a new owner,
Christ Jesus, the atoner.
Now, my soul belongs to God;
My path is the one that Jesus trod.

There will be times that I fail.
My feet will surely leave the trail.
But I know I'll never turn back,
No matter how hard you attack.

Your power is truly gone …
As surely as break of dawn,
After an awful, stormy night,
When no hope seems in sight.

4. Not What I'd Pictured

It's not exactly what I'd hoped for,
Not exactly what I'd planned,
Not exactly what I'd pictured in my mind …
When I said, Lord I resign.
Take my life in your hands,
Lead me on to the Promised Lands.

It's not exactly what I'd hoped for,
Not exactly what I'd planned,
Not exactly what I'd pictured in my mind …
But I like it anyway.
No more guilt, no more shame.
No more shifting around blame.

It's not exactly what I'd hoped for,
Not exactly what I'd planned,
Not exactly what I'd pictured in my mind …
But the peace of mind is worth it.
Jesus Christ in my life
Helps me work through grief and strife.

5. Why the Tears?

Why the tears?
When no one's around
To hear you cry …
Why the tears?

Why the tears?
When you know in your heart
That the Lord is near …
Why the tears?

Dry those tears.
And remember the Lord
Is always there.
Dry those tears.

Dry those tears.
And lean on the promises
Of the King.
Dry those tears.

6. Speak Soft Words
(Also in *Heartfelt Cases 1: The Collins Case*)

So, here I am again,
Baffled and confused,
Come before you, Lord God.
Saying …
Please give me wisdom.
Please give me wisdom.
For my head is pounding
With the problems of the world around me.
Won't you, please give me wisdom.
Won't you, lead my heart today, Lord.

So, here I am again,
Worn and weary,
Come before you, Lord God.
Saying …
Speak soft words to me, Lord.
Speak soft words to me.
For my ears are ringing
With the loud shouts of the world around me.
Won't you speak soft words to me, Lord.
Won't you speak soft words today.

Totally at peace.
That is where I'll be
When the Lord God is near.

7. My Days are Numbered
(Also in *Heartfelt Cases 2: The Kiverson Case*)

My days are numbered,
And I don't know that number.
But I thank God for every breath I take,
For every moment He's seen fit to grant me.
This I do know: I'm in good hands.

My days are numbered,
And I don't know that number.
But I thank my God for every day
Of this life, I oft take for granted.
This I do know: I'm in good hands.

My days are numbered,
And I don't know that number.
But I know God knows,
And that's a comfort in trying times.
This I do know: I'm in good hands.

8. No Sleep

Why can't I sleep tonight?
You'd think I'd never thought a single thought
And had to make up for it all tonight.
Why can't I sleep tonight?

I cannot sleep tonight.
My mind is racing to a land of dreams.
It races to a world full of worries.
I cannot sleep tonight.

Lord, help me sleep tonight.
For only You can Solve my problems,
Only You can set my mind at ease.
Lord, help me sleep tonight.

9. Times of Trouble
(Also in *Heartfelt Cases 3: The Davidson Case*)

So, it seems like your world
Is falling apart all around you.
Tell me, what will you do?
Where will you go?
And who can you turn to in times of trouble?

There are several ways to answer all these.
The best thing to do in times of need
Is to fall to your knees,
For the best place to be when you can't go on,
Is in the arms of your Heavenly Father.

So, it seems like your world
Is falling apart all around you.
Tell me, what will you do?
Where will you go?
And who can you turn to in times of trouble?

God's the only one who can make you strong
Enough to stand against the world.
With His holy help,
You will make it through each fiery trial,
With your heart and mind yet whole.

So, when it seems like your world
Is falling apart all around you.
I say, fall to your knees
And seek out the Lord,
And he will help you in times of trouble.

10. Is There Anything …

I want to shout to all the world
That God is the Lord over all.
I want ask them all this:
Is there anything more beautiful
Than the sight of a star-studded night
That heralds to all the world,
Just how much God cares for the details?

I know that things go wrong,
But God is always there.
I want to ask you one more thing:
Is there anything more wonderful
Than the peace of mind that comes
From knowing God knows
Everything that goes on around you?

11. Walk On

There is peace in my life.
There is hope in my life.
There is joy in my life.
There is strength in my life because …
God has given me peace.
God has given me hope.
God has given me joy.
God has given me strength to walk on.

In the strength of the Lord,
I will walk on through trials,
I will walk on through pain,
I will walk on through whatever comes my way.

Long ago, God did say,
When you're weak then you're strong.
When is seems like you can't go on,
Call on God and you will
Always find strength to walk on.

In the strength of the Lord,
You will walk on through trials,
You will walk on through pain,
You will walk on through whatever comes your way.

12. God Will have the Last Word
(Also in *Heartfelt Cases 1: The Collins Case*)

As the world falls apart me around me,
I think of this truth and peace comes:
God will have the last word.
He has in ages past, He still does today,
And the future's certain when it comes to this:
God will have the last word.
Our Mighty King came to Earth
As a baby, to live and love and die,
But that wasn't the end by far,
Jesus had the last word when He rose again!

13. Beautiful Day

The beauty of this day is not lost on me.
The sun is shining brightly.
The sky is a pretty shade of blue,
And there are fluffy little white clouds
Soaring on the wings of the same wind
That plays with my hair.
O the care, O the detail, O the thought
That went into designing this world!
It's a humbling, comforting thought to see
That God's so much bigger than me.

I know I have much to do today,
But I can't help but stop
I can't help but stop and enjoy,
The beauty of the world around me.
A thousand dreary days are worth it to
Enjoy the full measure of the beauty of this day.
O the care, O the detail, O the thought
That went into designing this world!
It's a humbling, comforting thought to see
That God's so much bigger than me.

There's a sense of peace that comes
And surrounds my heart when I realize that
The same God who created that sun,
The same God who painted that sky,
The same God who designed those clouds,
Is the same God who rules my life.
O the care, O the detail, O the thought
That went into designing me!
It's a humbling, comforting thought to see
That God's so much bigger than me.
O, the beauty of this day is not lost on me.

14. Deep-seated Peace

There may not be overflowing joy
Coming out of me but I know
There's a deep-seated peace hiding in me.
Look deep in my eyes.
Can you see the deep-seated peace hiding in me?
What's that?
You say you can't see the peace …
Oh well,
I know there's a deep-seated peace hiding in me.
It flows from the fountain of life
That sprang up when I accepted Christ.
So though you may not see
The deep-seated peace hiding in me,
All can see the source of that peace.
It is Christ the Lord who reigns on high.
So come and accept him and receive
The deep-seated peace hiding in me.

15. Am I Hiding My Heart?

When you look at me what do you see?
Do you see a fire to serve the Lord?
Or am I hiding my heart deep inside?

Every good thing comes from the Lord my God.
I am so blessed, but how can I share,
The many good things God has given to me?
From this day on, I will walk by faith,
Trusting that I am under grace.

When you look at me what do you see?
Do you see a fire to serve the Lord?
Or am I hiding my heart deep inside?

Do you know the things that haunt my dreams?
I fear to fail, I fear to fall,
But most of all, I fear I fail to do.
My own salvation's not the issue here.
What is, is that I'm here and the lost are there.

When you look at me what do you see?
Do you see a fire to serve the Lord?
Or am I hiding my heart deep inside?

16. Rain Down Wisdom

I wish I were perfect,
But I know that cannot be
This side of Heaven.
So here I am, my Father,
On my knees, begging you please
Rain down wisdom on me.

O I know my salvation's sure,
From the very day I surrendered.
In You, I know, I am strong,
But there are times when I am so weak
Deep down inside of me.
So here I am, my Father,
On my knees, begging you please
Rain down wisdom on me.

The many sides of me are at war
Trying to grab pieces of my heart.
Lord, I meant what I said, when I said,
"My heart is yours."
So won't you please
Rain down wisdom on me.

Teach me how to be a servant.
Teach me how to be a friend.
Teach me how to praise you properly.
Here I am, Father,
On my knees, begging you please
Rain down wisdom on me.

17. Every Moment

Every moment is a gift,
Though it may not seem that way.
Even trials have their place
As they teach us to pray:
"Father God, rain down peace over me
For I am struggling through life today."

Every moment is a gift,
Though it may not seem that way.
Think of all the good things in your life.
Have you neglected to say:
"Father God, thank you for blessing me
All of these days and in all of these ways …"?

Every moment is a gift,
Though it may not seem that way.
So cherish every moment
And continue to pray:
"Father God, teach me to follow your ways
For I am your servant all of my days."

18. Worry Won't Win Any Wars

It seems like this life is one tiny war after another.
Whether they be mental, spiritual, physical, emotional,
At some point you're gonna have to fight them.

What weighs heavily upon your mind?
Are you worried that you can't pay your bills?
Are you worried that you can't feed your kids?
Are you worried that that person close to you
Doesn't seem to love you?
Are you worried?
Do not worry,
For worry won't win any wars right now.

What weighs heavily upon your mind?
Are you worried 'cause you just failed that test?
Are you worried 'cause you haven't got a job?
Are you worried 'cause your best friend's father died
And you just don't know what to say?
Are you worried?
Do not worry,
For worry won't win any wars right now.

When you get a free moment open a Bible
Find your strength in the written word.
As for the spiritual war raging around us,
The weapons to win this war were given to us long ago.
When you get a free moment open a Bible
Find your answers in the written word.
Though worry won't win any wars right now,
We have a heavenly Father who cares.
So when you get a free moment open a Bible
And find your peace in the written word.

19. Driving Me Crazy

Worry is driving me a little bit crazy.
Maybe I spoke too hastily,
Maybe I didn't think this through …
No, I know I didn't think this through.
So what am I gonna do?
'Cause worry is driving me a little bit crazy.

O I know it won't do any good.
But I cannot help it
'Cause it just plain comes.
O I know God's got it all in hand,
And I know that things will be all right.
But worry's still driving me a little bit crazy.

Lord, come and be my help tonight.
Come and be my peace of mind.
Come and be my sanity …
'Cause worry is driving me a little bit crazy.

20. Freely

Freely ye have received the good news
That Jesus came to save all this world.
So freely give to those around you,
The hope that you have hiding inside.
Declare everywhere who you are,
A son or daughter of the one King,
The High King of Heaven.

Fear not what they may think
For they must hear that God loves them.
No one will ever escape from the truth
That all will perish without the Lord.
But there is hope in our Holy Father,
The one King, the High King, God in Heaven.

Freely ye have received this good news
So freely give to all those around you.
There are so many in this world who are hurting.
Tell them by speaking, show them by doing.
Let them see Christ shining.
Let them see how wonderful it is to truly be free.

21. Listen

Do I speak too much?
Should I pray more?
Should I listen more?
All too often I am too busy
Crying out, "O God hear my plea …"
That I'm not listening for His answer.
Then, I wonder why I receive no reply,
When I'm not listening
'Cause I'm too busy complaining
Of all the things that befall me.

O Father, speak to me tonight.
I've come to listen to You.
Come and teach me the meaning
Of a quiet time with You.
Come and teach my heart to listen.
For long ago, I mastered the art
Of telling You every problem on my mind,
But I forgot to listen.
So teach me how to listen …
For Your words of comfort and wisdom.

22. Better

What makes the life of a Christian any better?
Are we better than anybody else?
Not by a long shot, not even close.
No one is better than anybody else,
And no one will ever be good enough.
Hence, the reason for the grace of God.
Hence, the reason for Christ's sacrifice
At the cross to redeem this fallen world.

What makes the life of a Christian any better?
Are we better off than anybody else?
Yes, we are better off than all those
Who do not have the Lord
To lean on in times of trouble.
For though today may be hard,
We can know that tomorrow will be better,
And even if it's not, we can still rejoice.
For hard times will only make it
That much sweeter when our broken hearts
Finally make it to Heaven's perfect peace.

23. Dancing Sun

See the sun dance with joy.
Yesterday, and the day before, it rained,
Making it hard to see beauty all around.
But today the clouds have run,
Revealing a clear blue sky.
See the sun shining forth,
Bouncing to and fro off everything,
O it's quite a sight!

Everything revealed by light looks better.
See the sun; it dances there
Making things look happier.
Come take a walk with me,
And we'll watch the sun dance.

Just as things look better by light,
So God's love shining through
Reveals the best inside of you.
Let God's love shine through
So they may see what they could have.
Invite them all to take a walk
To see the dancing sun.
Then, share the Kingdom of the Son.
Some will see the truth and be saved.

Everything revealed by light looks better.
See the sun; it dances there
Making things look happier.
Come take a walk with me,
And we'll watch the sun dance.

24. Made to Praise

As I walked around on this gorgeous day,
I reflected on my life and then prayed,
"Father God, thank you for being You.
Thank you too for the many blessings …
I would try to count them,
But they are countless.
Thank you for being holy …
All good things in life reflect You …"

At that moment I realized …
You and I, we were made
To praise His name.
You and I, we were made
To love and be loved.
You and I, we were made
To live, learn, grow, and pray.
You and I, we were made
To lift our hands, bow our hearts,
And open our eyes to the truth.
We were made to praise the Lord!
We were made to praise Him!

25. Peace of God

Peace of God reign in me
Help me see Your glory.
It's like a crown to be found
On everything around,
But I cannot see it today!

Peace of God reign in me
Help me see Your glory.
For only You are Lord Most High.
Only You can satisfy
Every desire of my heart.

Peace of God reign in me
Help me see Your glory.
For I am scared of today,
And what tomorrow may bring my way.
Wrap me in Your peace.

Peace of God reign in me
Help me see Your glory.
For only with my eyes on You
Will I be brought through
Every trial I must face.

Peace of God reign in me
Help me see Your glory.
For only You can give me peace
May I never ever cease
Praising Your holy name!

26. Right Place to Sing

I sing in the shower, don't you?
I sing in the car, don't you?
I sing on the way to class, don't you?
I sing almost anywhere
For almost anywhere is the
Right place to sing
Praises to the King.

I sing as I take a walk.
I sing as I stand in line.
I sing in the grocery store.
I sing almost anywhere
For almost anywhere is the
Right place to sing
Praises to the King.

I do get a few strange looks,
But I don't really care,
I say, "Let them stare …"
All they'll see is me
Singing praises to my King.
I am practicing for Heaven
Where everywhere will be the
Right place to sing
Praises to the King!

27. Light in My Eyes

Let there always be a light in my eyes
For it speaks of love for this life.
I am eager to learn the things
God has in store for me.
Though things may change,
For now I am at peace.

Let there always be a light in my eyes
For it reflects God's Word in me.
All good things come from God's hands.
Though evil abounds all around
We can know God's promise
To set things right in the end.

Let there always be a light in my eyes
For it shows the hope within.
As long as the Light lives in me,
I live in the Light
And the Light dispels all darkness.
I will find peace in the Light.

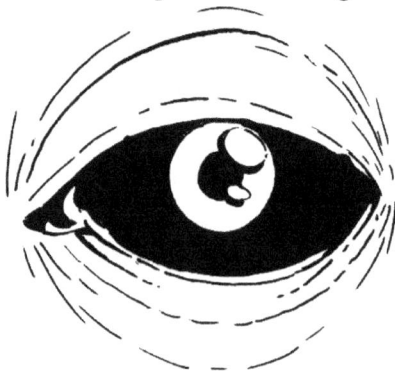

28. We Needed a Hero

We needed a hero
And God provided well.
Though I can barely fathom it,
I sure do believe:
The wrath of God has no remedy.
The grace of God knows no bounds.
How can this be?

We needed a hero
And God provided well.
I have felt the grace of God.
And the Bible is filled
With tales of wrath.
Yet with tales of wrath
Come tales of grace.

There is no greater tale
Than the true account of Jesus's life.
We needed a hero
And God provided well.

29. Chosen One

I know the Chosen One.
He is my friend.
Let me tell you all about Him.
He is holy, mighty, just,
Wonderful in every way.
He is loving, kind, gentle,
And powerful in every way.

I know the Chosen One.
He is my friend.
I'm going to praise His name!
He is the Counselor, Prince of Peace,
Lord over all things.
He is the Shepherd, perfect Judge,
And Defender of all.

I know the Chosen One.
He is my friend.
I will strive to be like Him.
He has mastered all things admirable,
And saved the lives of many.
He is the Chosen One;
I am a messenger.
Let us strive to be like Him!

30. Move, Mountain, Move

So long I've gone this journey
Walking in a land full of lost.
I see their pain clear as day
And I have the soothing answer.
Wish that they would know my Lord.
Such would be sweet to my soul.
He is peace brought to life.
He sought not His will but
Submitted to death for all.
My soul weeps at the word of the Lord
"All fall short of the glory of God."
And again, I weep, this time for joy,
Knowing God sent Christ for you and me.
It seems so long since I last spoke
On behalf of those like me.
They are stubborn in heart,
Solid as mountains set in their ways.
God's been known to shake the earth
To move a mountain where He pleases.
I would not wish ill on anyone,
But if it saves their soul,
Maybe shaking's the way to go.
I have faith so I'll say,
"Move, Mountain, move!"

31. End and Beginning

End of a day, beginning of a new
Here I am trying to think.
Some profound thought lies
On the edge of my imagination.
I can almost feel it.
Something weighs on my heart.
It feels like it was made of lead.
Lord, move heart and mind.
Bring me to the point where I can say
"I picked up my cross today,
And I was glad."
Many times, I carry on Christian duty,
Looking like somebody just died.
I contemplate good acts,
Sigh, and think, "I suppose I'll help
For it's what Christ would do."
Well, it's a good thing God forgives
And uses us despite false motives!
I cried out and my eyes were opened.
It's the end of a day, beginning of a new …

32. Best Day

There's a gray cast to the sky today.
Rain hangs in the air like a mystery.
Will it come today or tomorrow?
Does it matter either way?
All things happen in God's time.
Impatient as I am, the days slip by
And I can't reclaim a one.
These are the best days of life they say,
But I'm starting to see
Every day in God's arms,
Learning from the Holy One,
Is the best day of my life.
How humbling, how amazing to know
God knows each small flame.
I am one in ten trillion
How can it be that God knows me?
Such a thing lies far beyond my thoughts,
But He's good and I know He knows
Everything that shall come to pass.
Won't you come and join this family.
Then today and every day, good or ill,
Will be the best day of your life!

33. Let Him In

There's a stranger knocking at your door.
Don't be scared; don't be shy.
Open that door; let Him in.
He's the most patient man there ever was.
He won't shout; He won't curse
But he just might cry.
After all, it's for you He sacrificed.
He's not going away; let Him in.
You can drown the knock with noise.
You can stand behind the barricades.
You can huddle down and close your eyes.
But you can't wait forever,
For you might not have that time.
Just try to face the fact:
He's not going away.
Let Him in.

34. Dance to Life

I've got a tune in my head,
Slippery as a ball of grease.
Can't keep track of it.
It goes where it wants to.
High or low or somewhere in between.
I remember now, but wait a moment
I'll probably lose it just like before.

It's kind of bouncy.
Dang, I'll be up tonight.
I feel like dancing.
Won't you dance with me?
What shall we dance to?
How about life?

35. The Long Story

The past is the past and unchangeable.
The future is there to be redefined.
I suppose you could say,
"Every day was written long ago,
So why try to change?"

Life may be one long story,
Part comedy, part tragedy,
But the way this script was written
We have a choice to be
Hero, villain, or victim.
At times, we play all three.
We cannot control much,
But that's the adventure.

Heroes are made every day.
Until they breathe their last,
Anyone can change.
What's holding you back?
Everyone has their trials.
Heroes simply rise above.
How will your story end?

36. Never Alone

The loss is deep; the pain is sharp.
You cry out into dark
"Nobody knows my pain!"
Hate to contradict the hurt,
But you're not alone out here.
When darkness falls and all seems lost
Turn to the Holy One.
Cry upon God above.
He's the only one who can
Take that pain and fling it far,
Pour soothing peace until you rest.
Best of all, He loves you.
He died to rise and conquer sin.
Though we still feel its blow,
We can always know He knows.
He will walk each hard step.
He will share in love and pain.
You are never alone.

37. Somewhere Today

Somewhere today somebody died.
Maybe he was a soldier carrying out his duty.
Maybe she was a child succumbing to disease.
Maybe he thought nobody cared,
So he took his own life.
Maybe she was a mommy
Somebody's gonna miss.
Somewhere today somebody died,
And somewhere today somebody's crying,
"Is this all there is to life,
A series of steps towards a hungry grave?"
I refuse to believe that this is all.
I have seen and heard too many miracles.
Every discovery, self-revelation, and peaceful
Moment is a gift from God
Who is just and full of grace.
We are weak and prone to fail,
But somewhere today somebody's learning.
Maybe he took his first step.
Maybe she passed that tough test.
Maybe he saw how she loves him.
Maybe somewhere today somebody
Finally surrendered their life to God.
Maybe somewhere today somebody's finally living.

38. Grim Day

This day didn't start so well,
Pouring rain and looking o so grim.
Had to remind myself God promised
Not to drown the world again.
Still no sun to be found here, but
At least the clouds are much less menacing.
I'd say consider each raindrop
Isn't it neat, but then
I'd just be lying to you.
Ever notice we have a tendency
To focus on irrelevant things?
People die every day
Never knowing Christ saves.
They had their chance to make a choice.
Do not miss yours too.
If you know the King then declare it.
There's nothing to fear.
Though this day didn't start out so well,
It turned out all right.
Life is full of storms,
But my God is full of grace.

39. Lost Ones

Are you a lost one?
I know that sounds strange,
But are you a lost one?
My Master sent me out on a journey
To find all the lost ones
Who knew not the way.
Are you a lost one?
Are you waiting for someone
To find you out here alone in this cold?
Are you a lost one?
Well, no matter, I've found you at last.
Come with me we'll have a party.

Won't you come home with me?
Don't you see?
The Master's arms are always
Open to the lost ones.
That is, you and me, we're one family.
Once torn apart by sin and shame,
Now united through Christ.
Won't you celebrate with me?
We're lost no more!
Praise the Lord God,
We're lost no more!

40. New Title

God walk with me on this journey,
For I know not the way to go.
As you guide me, I will conquer
Doubt, fear, despair, and pain.
Though this world may be fallen,
Your beauty shines everywhere.
Stars that shine only at night,
Newborn babies sleeping softly,
Trees clothed in leaves and light,
All declare You are here.
God You reign forevermore.
Thank you for this life.
Thank you for being holy.
All that power, all that glory,
All cast down to save the lost.
Chief of sinners once my title,
Stripped away by saving grace,
Slave to sin or servant of God,
I have chosen my place.
I'll declare it out loud.
My new title: child of God.

41. Money Can and Cannot

Money cannot buy peace of mind.
Money cannot buy happiness.
Money cannot buy lasting love.
Well, what good is it?

The quest for money has claimed many lives.
Abuse and hate have claimed many more.
Universal goals of love and peace
Get forgotten when money is at stake.
The rich and famous may live all right,
But thousands die every day from poverty.
Can money solve this problem?

Money may ransom a rich man's life,
But it put him in danger in the first place.
Money may buy a short-term cure,
But will it save your soul?
Money may buy food for a day.
By tomorrow you'll be hungry.

Money cannot buy peace of mind.
Money cannot buy happiness.
Money cannot buy lasting love.
Is it worth dying for?

42. God Doesn't Know How to Fail

Went to church just the other day.
Heard Joseph's tale told in a new way.
Heard how he was sold as a slave,
Wrongly accused, thrown into jail,
Forgotten by so many people
For so many years,
But not forgotten by God.
My God who doesn't know how to fail.

Wondered how this message applied to me.
Kept returning to this one point.
My God doesn't know how to fail.
I'm sure I fail many times,
Complain endlessly, fall on my face,
But I can always be sure
My God doesn't know how to fail.

43. Enemy

How many times have you heard the devil say,
"I'm not the enemy.
You won't get rid of me.
I'm not your enemy!
I have only your interests in mind."?

How many times have you echoed in your heart,
"I'm not the enemy.
Though evil surround me,
I will not be consumed.
I have only good in mind."?

When did you become an expert
At lying to yourself?
Don't you realize
You have become the enemy?
Evil has swallowed you whole.

Come back from darkness!
No evil is too great.
It is still not too late.
Turn from this destructive path
Or become your own worst enemy.

44. When You're Weary

When you're weary, when you're worried,
When this world's got you so low
The earth would have to open
To let you sink lower,
That's when you know for sure
You need Christ in your life.
Why wait 'til trouble comes?
Why wait 'til the ache in your heart gets
So bad you think it might just burst open wide
And scatter small pieces from shore to shore?

When you're weary, when you're worried,
Cry out to the Lord.
He will hear you. He will answer.
He will give you peace of mind.
Things still might not go right,
But you can know for sure
God will always be waiting
To catch your tears.
In Him, find rest, weary one.

45. Mountain of Troubles

There may be a mountain of troubles ahead,
But always remember you're never alone.
When you need strength look back and see
The many miracles manifest in thee.
God is forever gracious and true.
He will lead you day by day.
Take life one day at a time.
Tomorrow's got its own troubles.
No use borrowing more today.
Let His peace reign in you.
Then, no mountain of troubles
Can weigh your heart down.
There may be a mountain of troubles ahead,
But the Rock behind you is far greater.

46. Had Enough?

When nothing goes right and you feel so lost,
When everything's right and you still feel lost,
Ask yourself some questions.

Have you had enough?
Have you had enough of running your life?
Have you had enough of making mistakes?
Have you had enough of feeling lost?
Have you had enough?

Don't you think it's time you surrendered it all?
Don't you think it's time to say,
"God, I've had enough!
Take my life and make me more like You."

I'm not saying lightning's going to fall from the sky,
God's going to speak from the mountains,
Or anything of that nature,
But it's never happened in the course of history
Someone cried out, "Lord, help me!"
And didn't receive an answer.
Have you had enough?

47. About the Word

You'd think I'd know
My own heart by now,
But it confuses me every day.
Have I forgotten what it's like
To be a sinner under grace?
Have I forgotten how to ask
The Lord for daily wisdom?

Some songs make no sense to me.
When I pause to reflect,
I come to realize
Sometimes I think too hard.
It's not about the song at all.
It's about the Word and
The Word made flesh and
The Flesh that died and
The Man that rose again!
It's about the Word.

48. Refined by Fire

When it seems everything is going wrong,
Just hold on to this thought.
Every trial and tribulation
Is only a spark,
Merely a part of cleansing fire.
Refined by fire.
That's what I'll be.
If this trial don't break me,
It will make me into something better
Than I had ever imagined.

Out of this fire I'll walk unscathed
For fire can burn me, maybe break me,
But it can never take me away from God.
He's my comfort, my great provider.
When this world weighs on my heart,
I'll just try to remember
It's only a part of refining fire.
This trial can never break me long.
It can only make me stronger
By driving me closer to God.

Julie C. Gilbert

49. Beautiful, Magnificent

In ancient days, they looked
At the moon and stars,
Saw how beautiful, saw how magnificent,
And called them god.
I look at the moon and stars
See how beautiful, see how magnificent
And say, "Praise the Lord!
That sight is no accident.
All that is beautiful, all that is perfect
Is crafted by God."

All hail King Jesus!
He made the moon and stars.
He made you and me.
He made us truly free.
Can't help but stand and sing
All hail King Jesus!
He is beautiful, most magnificent,
And He is my God!

50. I've Heard it Said

About this time, I always think of my life.
Try to reconcile what I've done and will do.
There are several goals I have in mind.
I wonder if they're all my own.
I've heard it said, "You can't lose salvation."
Don't know if I believe my ears.
I've heard it said, "You can't lose salvation,"
But I know it's true
You can fall away from right.
Don't think I'm in much danger of that,
And that's probably where the trouble starts.
I've heard it said, "You can't lose salvation."
That may be true but you can sure fall far.
Falling may be the best thing,
But it sure ain't easy on the way down!
I've asked God to mold me like clay,
Then it crossed my mind:
Molding may be the best thing,
But sometimes it hurts like crazy.
I've heard it said, "You can't lose salvation."
True or not, I'll not lose mine.
Though the molding may break me,
I'll be better for the change.

51. Prayer for You

Heard you were down today.
Didn't know what to say,
So I started to pray.

God, you know my heart
And that I don't have words to start.
Please be with my friend.
Wrap your peace around her mind.
Help her with answers she seeks to find.
Let her know
Every pain helps us grow.
Life can seem without direction
Walking forth waiting for correction,
But you're no stranger to rejection.
Give her the strength to carry
Your love to those you would marry
Your heart to and call heirs
To your kingdom. Nothing else compares.

I found words to say
When I began to pray
May God work in your heart today.

52. All the Riches

Seeped in a world where everything
Can be bought or bartered for,
I'm amazed every time I realize anew:
All the riches of all the ages
Cannot purchase the freedom
I have so freely in Christ alone.
Freedom from thoughts and worries.
Freedom from tempting sins.
Shackles I had felt and never felt
Fell away one day,
And no matter how many times
I try to climb back into them
They will hold me no more.
All my money and other riches
Could not accomplish what one
Man's perfect life and death did.
All the riches of all the ages
Cannot purchase the freedom
I have so freely in Christ alone.

53. Sweetly Boundless

Like the oceans,
Clear night skies,
Thoughts that lay behind
Stormy eyes,
True love is sweetly boundless.
Some would take that to mean
Any one of a thousand things.
All I meant by what I said:
Truest love there ever was belonged to God.
Though I wander far away from the truth,
True love pursues my soul.
Some would call it foolishness.
Others would agree with me:
Love that would not spare the Son
Can only be seen as sweetly boundless.
All other loves fade with time.
Not my Jesus.
He's forever,
For His love is sweetly boundless.

54. Farewell

I was pondering how
To best say goodbye
When it crossed my mind
It's not really goodbye.
It's more like farewell
As in fare ye well for I might
Not see you for a long time,
Maybe not 'til the end of this age.
But if you know God
And I do too
And we both trust in Christ
To be our perfect sacrifice
There is no goodbye, only farewell
As in fare ye well for I might
Not see you for a long time.
So walk with God
And I will too
And when we meet again
We can share our many tales
Until then fare ye well.

55. Time for Good Cheer

Christmas comes but once a year.
O, what a time for good cheer.
Yet here we are running around,
Going half-crazy buying just one more thing.
We slap on a smile but complain inside.
"It's freezing cold and there's no sign of snow."
"The tree fell over twice …"
In the midst of the chaos
I must pause or lose my mind.
I try to remember.
Christmas comes but once a year.
It should be a time for good cheer.
The reason for this whole season is
Jesus Christ who gave up Heaven to
Ransom sinners from the fires of hell!
O, what a happy thought that is!
How many times have I given thanks
For such a priceless gift?
Christmas may be once a year
But with Christ in me
Every day's a time for good cheer!

Thin Black Road

56. Hard Side of Heaven

I've shed my share of tears
And I'll probably part with more.
Somewhere in this mess
I will find my peace.

It's always hard to be told
You're not good enough.

Some part of me is crying,
"Who's holding the standard?"
The other part of me knows
It doesn't really matter.
We're on the hard side of Heaven.

This is me broken.
This is me whole.
This is me finding the pieces
Somebody scattered.
This is me finding peace
In the One who crossed on over.
The same One who rules my life.

We may be on the hard side of Heaven.
But my help and hope can be found
In the pages of a Book,
In the God-shaped space in my soul.

57. Run Away

Wait!
Please hear me out!
I see you're running away again.
Though it is breaking me,
I won't stop you long.
Please just answer a few questions.
Is all this running really worth it?
Will the bottle help you understand?
Will the drugs drive away your pain?
I know you miss your father.
I sure do.
War's never easy but neither is life.
Think of all you leave behind
Every time you run away.
I've cried. I've begged. I've prayed
God would give us wisdom.
I have no profound words to say,
Only this promise:
No matter how many times you run away
I'll be waiting here for you.
You'll never cease to be my son.
Just remember God's not like me.
He will chase you. He will find you
No matter how far you run away.
Is all this running really worth it?

58. Sleep Softly

Go to sleep now. Dawn will come soon.
Go to sleep now. I'll be right here.
Go to sleep now. No need to fear.
Night and day, I will pray
One day, you will know the Lord.
One day, you will understand.
One day, you will make a choice.
Night and day, I will pray
You choose to follow God's way.
I wish I could fight your battles.
I wish I could make your choice.
I know I wish in vain.
I can guide you on the way,
But ultimately the choice remains yours.
The grace of God can save you.
One day, you will understand.
Until that day, do not worry.
Do not worry. God will watch you.
Do not worry. God will guide you.
Until that day, sleep softly.
Sleep softly, little one, God is with you.
Sleep softly, little one, God will guide you.
Sleep softly, little one, God loves you.

59. Keep Dreaming

Dreams are born in inspired moments
And last a lifetime.
Dreams lend strength to the hopeless,
Direction to the lost.
When you're weary,
Keep dreaming, keep hoping.
Hope will lead you through to a new day.
Maybe that day will be worse
Than the last one,
But it's a new day,
A day for new dreams,
Dreams with hope enough
To carry you through dark times.
When things get so bad
You think you might just snap in two,
Keep dreaming, keep hoping.
Hope will lend you strength to go on.
You will walk through your trials.
You will make it to a new day.
That new day may see your dreams come true.

60. Happy Birthday Anyway

So, you're one day older.
They say you're one year older.
That makes you sound so old.
Happy birthday anyway.
Don't focus on tomorrow.
Today's your special day.
Tomorrow you'll just be one day older.
Happy birthday anyway.
This year sure did go by.
The next will fly faster.
Take heart. You're aging well.
Happy birthday anyway.

61. Mere Mortals

Come gather around and I'll tell you a tale.
I'll tell you a tale of life,
Tell you a tale of death.
I'll tell you a tale
But the lesson you learn is up to you.

While mere mortals slept out beneath the stars,
Tucked in tiny tents in neat little rows,
The spirits crept between them
And whispered in their ears.
"Dear mortal, I hope you sleep well.
Tomorrow comes far too soon
Bringing war, strife, and death
To friend and foe alike.
The battles rage around you
With Death winning every one.
You never know when the day's dawn
Will be the last dawn you see
So live your life accordingly.
Make calm moments, short letters, sweet smiles
The substance of your dreams.
Sleep well, dear soldier,
Tomorrow comes far too soon
Ye have not long to be a mere mortal."

62. Cricket's Destiny

Once alive
Now no more.
I crossed this earth
Singing summer songs
Softly.

The end came
Swift and sure
Before I had the time
To cry out why.

Wish
I had just
One more moment
To live.

63. Soldiers Make Good Promises

When I heard the news,
I cried out "Why?
Why, O God, let that good man die?
Accidents happen every day,
But why take the father of a little girl
So soon after losing her mother?"

Hardest thing I ever had to do was
Hold that little girl, hear her cry,
Feel her shake, and find the strength to say,
"Dear LeAnn,
It's okay to cry.
You don't know me,
But my name's Jim.
I know you feel all alone.
Come, take my hand.
In your parents' absence,
I'll do my best to raise you well,
Just as I promised I would."

Did your daddy ever tell you
Soldiers make good promises?
Did your daddy ever tell you
That your mommy was a soldier?
Did he ever tell you how
She died for me?
I am quite convinced
She set my soul free.

For some reason far beyond me
She chose to be my friend.

Julie C. Gilbert

I remember the day she died.
Though the sun was blazing,
The desert heat couldn't shake her smile.
The convoy had gone well
Until the shots rang out,
And we got out to fight.
At her orders, grunts like me fell into line.
We fought hard and fared well,
But the enemy had higher ground.

Did your daddy ever tell you
That your mommy was a soldier?
Did he ever tell you how
She set my soul free?

Hunkered down behind a pile of sand,
I found myself next to her.
She flashed a smile and shouted,
"God is in control!"
I replied with something vile.
She just ignored me.
I'll never forget her steady blue eyes
As she calmly replied,
"One day you will believe."

Did your daddy ever tell you
That your mommy was a soldier?
Did he ever tell you how she
Took three bullets for me?

Before I could catch my breath,
A man stood before us, rifle ready.
My hands froze, my shots went wide.

Thin Black Road

His first bullet grazed my head.
The next three marked for me found her instead.
Now pinned beneath her, I could only watch.
Somewhere she found strength to shoot.
That man never knew what hit him.

Did your daddy ever tell you
That your mommy was a soldier?
Did he ever tell you her
Last words to me concerned you?

With her dying breath, she spoke softly,
"Jim, you will know the Lord.
He has spoken to me.
Tell Tom I love him.
Soon, he will join me.
Take good care of my little girl.
Help her find the way."

That day, I made a promise
To care for you until I die.

Did your daddy ever tell you
That your mommy was a soldier?
Did he ever tell you
Soldiers make good promises?

64. Good and Better

I am well aware I am only one,
But you are one as well.
If you hear this cry for help—
That's good.
If you hear and add your voice—
That's better.
I believe in a land that's greater.
I believe in a time without fear.
I believe you and I can change
This whole world one soul at a time.
I am well aware I am only one,
But you are one as well.
If you and I raise our voices—
That's good.
If someone hears and joins—
That's better.
Our differences may be great,
But I know we both agree on this:
We believe in a time without fear.
We believe in a land where hearts
Are cradled and cherished—not broken.
And we can change this whole world
One soul at a time.

65. Dancing by the Sea

Daddy, do you remember
How it used to be when
There were three in this family?
Sure, we didn't have much,
But we had it all!
We'd save for months and rise at dawn
Just to go dancing by the sea.
Mommy would hold me,
You would hold her, and
With nothing but the sea birds watching,
We'd all go dancing by the sea.
Seems like such a long time
Since I lost you both to one fool
Going the wrong way on a one way.
The bottle won't fix this,
But one thing just might …
Mommy may still be gone,
But the sea's still there
And there are lots more birds to see us
Can we go dancing by the sea?

66. Somewhere a Song Plays

Somewhere a song plays for you,
Plays for me, plays for what we
Used to be.
I've known no sweeter time
Than the days spent with you,
Learning and living and breathing
Deeply of the peace that indwells you.
Lies came between us
And then a war.
Now I'm not sure of most things,
But one thing I know for sure:
My greatest lie was saying
I held no love for you.
I played the fool, but senses returned
So, I sought you to ask:
Can you hear that sweet melody?
Can that melody mend you and me to we?
Somewhere a song plays for you,
Plays for me, plays for what we
Used to be.

67. Distant Dreams

I am hard pressed to find
A future satisfying to my soul.
Distant dreams lie beyond me
Like a ribbon, bonny blue,
Tied to a far-off signpost.
I can see it waiving gaily,
Drawing my eyes to that sign,
But that cruel sign's many symbols
Refuse to explain my dreams.
As I draw ever nearer,
Seems that message is never clearer.
Distant dreams lie beyond me
Like a ribbon, bonny blue
Tied to a far-off signpost.
Am I doomed to forever follow
These distant dreams?

68. Tell Me Your Story

Behind every young man or woman
Lies a story waiting to be told.
Tell me your story.
Where did you come from?
What have you experienced?
Where are you going?
These are some of life's
Big questions.
Funny how it's easy to not see
How amazing life can truly be.
So, tell me your story.
What makes you smile?
What makes you laugh or cry?
What do you fear most of all?
Who are you trying to please?
What are your life goals?
Whatever your story may be
There is much more to tell.
So, tell me your story thus far.
Maybe we'll write something new.

69. The World is You

If you wish to kill me, walk away swiftly,
For my whole world is you.
The fire in every star
Cannot compare to you.
The light of life shines so bright
The rocks near come to life.
Don't you know, the world is you?

If you wish to kill me, walk away swiftly,
For my whole world is you.
See and hear the angels sing
They will tell you sweetly
All the gods bound to good
Are manifest in you.
Don't you know, the world is you?

If you wish to kill me, walk away swiftly,
For my whole world is you.
I could be blind and deaf
Yet still feel the good in you.
You haunt my dreams and my heart.
Please tell me we'll never part.
Don't you know, the world is you?

70. This Promise is Forever

At nighttime and all times,
My thoughts dwell with you.
Tell me you'll love me forever.
I could not take a parting, now or ever.
It would break my heart completely,
Shatter my mind, and turn my soul dark.

I am yours; you are mine.
This promise is forever.

You hold my heart in your hands
As you hold my soul with your smile.
Your eyes speak your mind and heart,
But I need to hear the words again.
Tell me you'll love me forever.
Then come what may, life will be perfect.

I am yours; you are mine.
This promise is forever.

I finally found what it means to love
Someone so much it hurts
At the thought of an end.
Tell me you'll love me forever.
I'll be all right though trials or pain
As long as I know I have you.

I am yours; you are mine.
This promise is forever.

71. Hero of My Dreams

You're the hero of my dreams,
But you're a stranger.
You're the hero of my dreams,
But I know you through legends alone.
Savior of Calveron, Red Knight,
Lousy Husband, Absent Father,
Hero to all but family.

You're the hero of my dreams,
But I know nothing of the real you.
I'm told I share your blood,
Fiery hair, and fearsome temper.
I know we both loved
The kindest woman who ever walked here.
I know you didn't kill her,
But you might as well have.
You gave her me, then broke her heart
To save some foreign city.

I'm told our sacrifice means something,
But I can't fathom what.
How can you be the hero of my dreams
When my soul only cries, "Villain"?

72. In My Dream

I saw you in a dream.
I saw you sitting here beside me,
Whispering all the good things life can offer.
It wasn't you as you are.
It wasn't you as you used to be.
There was something strange and wonderful
About this new you.

I saw you in a dream.
I saw you standing here before me,
Ice clinging to your heart and soul.
Something about the sight of broken me
Melted the ice and set you free.

I saw you in a dream.
I saw you standing here before me,
Hiding in the shadows,
Caught between desire and uncertainty,
Radiating pain and pleasure,
Wondering how you could comfort me.

I saw you in a dream.
I saw you sitting here beside me,
Whispering all the good things life can offer.
It wasn't you as you are.
It wasn't you as you used to be.
There was something strange and wonderful
About this new you.

In my dream, I beckoned.
It was more like a plea.

Thin Black Road

In my dream, you rushed forward.
In my dream, you dropped to your knees,
Took me by the hand, lifted my chin,
And wiped away the tears
With naught but a thumb and a grin.
In that moment, all the troubles of the past,
All I see in the future faded,
And I felt safe and whole again.

73. You Haunt My Dreams

Would you believe me if I told you
I cannot tell you how much I love you?
My heart, mind, and soul belong to you.
You cause me pain. You cause me joy.
You haunt my dreams, night or day.

No matter how long I know you,
I'm always learning something new.
Your eyes tell a story I want to hear,
And beg me to tell mine without fear.
Every moment spent apart
Breaks off a piece of my heart.

If I searched this whole world over,
I could not a find a love quite like you.
You make me feel safe, loved, and cherished.
Come and dance with me. Forget your worry.
Tonight belongs to you and me.

Would you believe me if I told you
I cannot tell you how much I love you?
My heart, mind, and soul belong to you.
You cause me pain. You cause me joy.
You haunt my dreams, night or day.

74. Pain I Cannot Ease

It is true.
Life is hard.
No doubts there.
Pain in me I can release.
Pain I see yet cannot touch
Weighs upon my heart.

It's not easy to feel pain.
Worse by far in some ways
Is watching one I love suffer
Pain I cannot ease.

Lord, please hear my heart's cry:
Let me not fail again.
My strength is not enough.
I need You to work in me
Miracles of small moments.

I'm not used to helplessness.
Give me grace to face each day.
Let Your love shine in me.

All these pains I cannot ease
Let me know I'm not perfect,
So, let me be more like You.

75. Fount of Life

The sun fades with flames,
Bright as a new day,
Promise of things to come.
There's sadness and hope here,
Feeling the fire slowly slip away.

What shall I do now?
Where shall I go now?
These echoes remain from many prayers.
Each foray out on my own
Ends in disaster, swift and sure.
There's sadness and hope here,
Feeling the fire slowly slip away.

Come, dear Father, friend of my soul,
Come hold me as I slowly die.
May death to myself and selfish desires
Bring new life like dawn.
May hope spring forth, bright and clear,
For herein lies the fount of life.
There's sadness and hope here,
Feeling the fire slowly slip away.

76. Song of the Dead

Here we are once again,
Singing for the dead.
Here we are once again,
Lamenting life lost.
May this song carry
The dead up to rest.
May it be that when we fall
Someone will sing over our grave.
May it be that when we fall
Someone will carry us on wings
Made of sweet songs.
Then life will go on.

77. Gift of Time with Her

Last night, I dreamed of you.
That's not unusual,
But in this dream I saw
All the stars above.
They were frantic with worry,
Thinking they'd lost one of their own.

I said, "She's with me,
Safe in my arms,
And I'll praise all the heavens
For the gift of time with her.
She's more beautiful than life itself.
The peace I see as she sleeps
Slips softly over me.
I will raise her to know
That the place she left behind
Remembers her fondly,
And we who see her as she is
Will praise all the heavens
For the gift of time with her."

78. The Teardrop
(Also in Nadia's Tears)

There are times when we
Ought to do more, you see?
Still there are times in this life
Filled with pain and much strife,
When the answers don't come clearly
And we wonder why we cling so dearly
To life lost and filled with so much cost
That leaves us feeling tempest tossed.
A search of the minds all around
For the answers to be found,
Led to many a question
And one conclusion:
There are times
Simply to
Cry.

79. Good Morning

It's a good morning.
Welcome, good morning.
Welcome, fine day,
One more chance to say
All you creatures great and small
Heed the morning call
Upon your heart to sing
It's a good morning.

It's a good morning,
Not one for mourning.
The past is past now.
There's no use wondering how
Your life slipped by so quickly.
So, I say to you truly
Release this year with not one tear.
Face the morning without fear.

It's a good morning.
Welcome, good morning.

80. Healer's Love

Should your ears fail to bear these words to you
Feel them with your spirit.
Let them write upon your heart.
Let them carry your soul to a place of safety.
I told you once my love is yours.
May you hear it many more.
Hard as it is to see you like this,
Please believe me when I say,
"A love like ours cannot be conquered this way."
Part of me feels, should you perish so would I,
If not in body, then in mind,
Yet I know I would go on living.
Just to carry the part of you at one with me.
If ever love had any power,
May it be enough to heal you.
I told you once my love is yours.
May you hear it many more.

81. Love Shall Find

Love shall find whom it will.
Dear father mine, need I remind?
You taught me what a man should be.
Strong, brave, kind, and truly free
To love, honor, serve, and save.
What matters his lowborn birth?

Love shall find whom it will.
Flee not, my love. Stand with me.
I hear their words and care not.
They hold no power over me.
Should they call for my crown
I would pay that price for you.

Love shall find whom it will.
Let learned men say otherwise.
From the way my heart cries
I know this love will pass
Test of time, trial of birth,
All reasons declaring it foolishness.

Love shall find whom it will.
I should know. It found me
When I wanted nothing more
Than to flee this strange new pain.
For the world I would gain,
I choose you and our love.

82. Best Way to Say Goodbye

Trying to find the best way to say goodbye,
Couldn't think of anything profound.
Maybe we'll meet again one day.
Maybe this is goodbye forever.
Either way, it's been a privilege
To know you day by day.
As you prepare to go away, I will pray
You will bless those you meet along the way.

If you learn nothing else from me,
Learn this and learn it well.
The secret to success in life is this
Find some way to serve someone else.
Then when you need some help
They'll be there, your best friend
Your spirit's guardian.
As you prepare to go away, I will pray
You will bless those you meet along the way.

Thank You for Reading:

I hope you enjoyed this first collection of Christian Inspirational Poetry. While reviews are awesome, let's do something different. If something in here touched you in anyway, share it with somebody else.

What does that mean? God has given everybody gifts. If you paint, paint. If you sing, sing. If you draw, draw. If you bake, bake, and so forth. Put the phrase or title or even a whole poem (if applicable) on your labor of love and use it to bless somebody.

It does not have to be shared on social media, and in some cases, it shouldn't. However, if you do, use #MTPchallenge if you choose to share via social media and tag me if you like. I'm on Facebook, Twitter, Instagram, and Mewe.

Hop on the **newsletter** if you want to keep up with life and new release news.
(https://www.subscribepage.com/n7e8l8)

Sincerely,

Julie C. Gilbert